Story by Sue Denim · Pictures by Dav Pilkey

THE BLUE SKY PRESS / AN IMPRINT OF SCHOLASTIC INC.   NEW YORK

To Abraham and Zippy —
Love, 'Momma Bunny'   S. D.

For Bonnie   D. P.

THE BLUE SKY PRESS

Text copyright © 1995 by Sue Denim
Illustrations copyright © 1995 by Dav Pilkey

For information regarding permission, please write to:
Permissions Department,
The Blue Sky Press, an imprint of Scholastic Inc.,
555 Broadway, New York, New York 10012.

The Blue Sky Press is a trademark of Scholastic Inc.

Library of Congress Cataloging-in-Publication Data
Denim, Sue, 1966–
The Dumb Bunnies' Easter / story by Sue Denim;
pictures by Dav Pilkey.   p.   cm.
Summary: It's December 24th, and the Dumb Bunnies are
celebrating the holidays in their own ridiculous way.
ISBN 0-590-20241-3
[1. Humorous stories.   2. Rabbits — Fiction.
3. Holidays — Fiction.]   I. Pilkey, Dav, 1966– ill.   II. Title.
PZ7.D4149Dv   1995   [E] — dc20   94-15050   CIP   AC

12 11 10 9 8 7 6 5 4 3 2 1   5 6 7 8 9/9 0/0
Printed in the United States of America   37
First printing, February 10, 1995
The illustrations in this book were done with watercolors,
India ink, acrylics, and Hamburger Helper.
Special thanks to Kevin Lewis.
Production supervision by Angela Biola
Designed by Dav Pilkey and Kathleen Westray

It was December 24th, and the Dumb Bunnies were getting ready for Easter.

Momma Bunny was stuffing the turkey,

Poppa Bunny was nailing up valentines…

...and Baby Bunny was giving eggnog
to a merry group of carolers.
"That's my boy," said Poppa Bunny.

Soon it was time for Poppa Bunny to go and pick out an Easter tree. So he put on his winter clothes and got ready to leave.

"Can I help you pick the Easter tree?" asked Baby Bunny. "I'm very good at picking things!"
"I can see that," said Poppa Bunny.

So Poppa and Baby Bunny went out and found
a wonderful tree. It was right in their neighbor's
front yard.

Poppa Bunny took out his saw and chopped
the tree down. Chop! Chop! Chop!

Then Poppa Bunny carried the Easter tree home.
(Baby Bunny helped a little bit.)

Later, Poppa and Baby Bunny put up the tree, while Momma Bunny brought three big boxes down from the basement.

"Now comes the fun part," said Momma Bunny.

"I get to put on the lights," said Poppa Bunny.
"I get to put on the ornaments," said Momma Bunny.
"And I get to put on the tinsel," said Baby Bunny.

So they did.

Then it was time for Thanksgiving
dinner, and everyone pitched in to help.
Poppa Bunny carved the turkey,
Momma Bunny tossed the salad...

…and Baby Bunny cut the cheese.
"That's my boy," said Poppa Bunny.

After supper, it was time for the Bunnies
to celebrate their dumb holiday traditions.

First, they painted Easter eggs.

Then they watched a little football
on the TV.

And finally, they ran to the fireplace
to hang up their stockings.

"Maybe we should have taken our stockings *off*, first," said Momma Bunny.

All night long, the Dumb Bunnies hung around and talked about the true meaning of Easter.

"I hope the Easter Bunny brings me a million dollars," said Momma Bunny.

"Oh, yeah?" said Poppa Bunny. "Well, *I* hope the Easter Bunny brings me a *THOUSAND* dollars!"

"I hope the Easter Bunny brings me a balloon," said Baby Bunny.

"Now don't be greedy," said Momma and Poppa Bunny.

"Sorry," said Baby Bunny.

That night while they slept, the Easter
Bunny came in a shiny red minivan...

...pulled by eight flying pilgrims.

The Easter Bunny gathered up dozens
of the most beautiful eggs he had...

...and dropped them down the chimney.
"Ho, ho, ho — look out below!" he yelled.

The next morning, the Dumb Bunnies were thrilled
to see what the Easter Bunny had brought them.

They had to admit that this was the most terrible Easter they had ever had...

...and they hoped their next Easter would be even *worse!*